Portraits
on Yellow Paper

Portraits
on Yellow Paper

Roddy Meagher and
Simon Fieldhouse

Central Queensland
UNIVERSITY
PRESS

First published in 2004 by Central Queensland University Press

Distributed by:
CQU Press
PO Box 1615
Rockhampton Queensland 4700
Ph: (07) 4923 2520
Fax: (07) 4923 2525
Email: cqupress@cqu.edu.au
www.outbackbooks.com

National Library of Australia

Cataloguing-in-Publication data:

Meagher, R. P. (Roderick Pitt), 1932- .
Portraits on yellow paper.

ISBN 1 876780 55 X (pbk.).

ISBN 1 876780 56 8 (hbk.).

1. Celebrities - Australia - Pictorial works.
2. Politicians - Australia - Pictorial works.
3. Lawyers - Australia - Pictorial works.
4. College teachers - Australia - Pictorial works.

I. Fieldhouse, Simon.

II. Title.

743.420994

Cover design and typesetting by Jane Dorrington
Printed and bound by Watson Ferguson & Co, Brisbane

Cover image of Roddy Meagher by artist Simon Fieldhouse

Please note:

CQU Press publishes this book in good faith after having performed due diligence about possible defamation and only after having received assurances from the author that the book is a playful jeu d'esprit, intended as imaginative jest and not as serious comment and that in real life Justice Meagher holds all the subjects in high regard.

The opinions of Justice Roddy Meagher are not necessarily those of Simon Fieldhouse

Contents

To the subjects of this book

Paddy Bergin

Paddy Bergin is formidable, strong, ruthless, undainty.

After obtaining her law degree, she became a solicitor at Messrs Stephen Jaques and Stephen, where she devoted her considerable skills to protecting the interests of commercial scoundrels who manufactured inedible bread out of permitted hours.

Then she transferred herself to the District Court and became Tutor to his Honour Judge Peter Ayrton Leslie.

When she went to the Bar of New South Wales, she first protected the medical profession of that state, and then organised secret police protection for Mr Justice Wood.

In gratitude, the State appointed her to be a Judge of the Supreme Court of New South Wales. There she still is.

Not long ago, she accepted an appointment to become Chief Justice of the Australian Capital Territory, later reneging on the deal. It is to be hoped that one day some investigative journalist will get to the bottom of this ugly incident.

She looks as if she plays golf. She does. She addresses the ball very firmly.

She distances herself from, and detests, the Women Lawyers' Association.

She is a good sort.

JUSTICE PATRICIA ANNE BERGIN

SIMON FIELDHOUSE 2004

Ian Callinan

Ian Callinan has now produced his fourth novel, and I am pleased to launch it.

How odd that a little civilization seeps out of the High Court. Callinan gives us plays and novels, and keeps adding to his enormous – and enormously valuable – art collection. His brethren don't. Sir Samuel Griffith wrote a translation of Dante; Mr Justice Gleeson did not. Imagine getting Justice McHugh to write a novel, even of the Guys and Dolls variety. Imaging squeezing a poem out of Justice Gaudron: if it came it would resemble, I have no doubt, Harold Pinter's famous poem in last year's *Spectator*. Imagine Justice Gummoff (aka Gummow) producing something creative – despite his foreign ancestry and manifest skills as a legal digester, so lacking is he in cultural literacy that he has never given birth to an epode or even a polished rune.

But I digress. Back to Callinan's novel. It concerns a group of uniformly unlovely people connected with a film. Its aging director Roderick Lily is holidaying on the Amalfi Coast. A bitchy journalist called Jane English pursues him, primarily to obtain a story on the alleged murder by him and his mistress of his wife, a story which led to a murder trial. Meanwhile, he is in trouble with his producer – or, rather, with both halves of his producer, a corporate giant. The majority shareholder – a crook – wants the production of his last film to be delayed as long as possible; the minority shareholder, another crook, wishes it to be accelerated. Scene follows scene – in Sydney, Brisbane, New York, London and Positano – with complexities mounting

IAN CALLINAN

SIMON FIELDHOUSE
2003

and deft character sketch following deft character sketch, until eventually the hero (if such he may be called) expires of motor neurone disease, an event which is thrilling for those who have insured him.

The tone of the book is genial, but not lacking in irony. It is dotted with good things. One of the production thugs on seeing a large carpet in an office said "It was made in India by young children", with a label on the back saying "No child labour used".

Or, again, consider this description of a chairman opening a meeting:

> *Kliner spoke slowly, as if he were introducing a country and western singer who needed no introduction.*

Or this:

> *Never worry about a lawyer pretending to be in a hurry since time charging became legal,* (If only "progressive" solicitors could read, and understand, this.)

These aphorisms adorn his tale, but (mercifully) point no moral.

The scenes describing the murder trial are realistic; there is none of that imaginary court procedure which Mortimer's "Rumpole" stories exhibit. As to his Honour's syntax and grammar, it is, as one might expect, only mildly peccable. "Footpath" is always used, correctly, instead of "pavement". There is but one split infinitive, although that is spoken by an Italian. "Firstly" appears twice, "St. James'" once. And, one cannot overlook the fact that, on no less than two occasions, the hero's coat is referred to as a "jacket" as if he were a potato. The non-word "receptioniste" is used once. And His unfortunate Honour has trouble with his singulars and plurals. Consider this sentence, for example: "Everyone involved in the production were prima donnas". Dot Wordsworth would not have approved.

What, then, is one's overall verdict? It is, in my view, a splendid novel; a credible, fast-moving tale. There are some who demand of a novel that it should be psychologically revelatory, others that it should be socially "relevant", or advocate some social or political cause; others that it be written in a stream of consciousness; others that it provide a sink of sexual lasciviousness in which one may wallow; and yet others that it be both pretentious and boring à la Patrick White and Christina Stead. It is none of these things. It is in the old tradition of being a non-doctrinaire, well-constructed, interesting, coherent and enjoyable narrative. No influence of Freud is evident. Nor of Marx, and little enough of James Joyce. That is what Trollope wrote, so did Barbara Pym and Elizabeth Taylor; so, for that matter, did Turgenev.

Ian Callinan has done remarkably well in this worldly tradition.

Edmund
Capon

Edmund Capon has been the Director of the Art Gallery of New South Wales for 25 years. Lucky, lucky New South Wales.

To gauge the extent of our luck, it is necessary to remember what the Gallery was like before he came on the scene.

To begin with, the Gallery was almost entirely empty of people, no matter when you went there. Perhaps there were a few derelicts who had wandered in from the park, and, if you were especially blessed, a handful of school-girls as well. Nowadays, more people attend the Gallery than they do cricket matches. (And this comparison will become even more true in the future if the Australian cricket team cannot do better than it did in the 2003-2004 Tests against India).

In the pre-Capon days, no really serious art was ever purchased. In those days, there were more regular purchases from England of portraits of admirals and generals, each looking like the other, and all looking like boiled codfish. Not until about 1925 was any European art ever bought, and when it was it was not of high quality. Since Capon arrived the Gallery has acquired major works of Henry Moore, Picasso, Kandinsky, Kirchner, Bonnard (twice), Degas, and others.

In the long reign of Hal Missingham, the main acquisitions were dreary oil paintings by his friend Tom Cleghorn.

To put his achievement in focus, it must be remembered to the eternal shame of both Labour and Liberal Governments, that the Gallery receives no public money to fund acquisitions. It means that the Director must perforce squeeze the funds out of private donors.

EDMUND CAPON

In the pre-Capon days, the directors were, to put it mildly, of little consequence: In fact, mediocrities. None of them had ever published any work of importance (whereas Capon has published quite extensively). None of them knew anything about Oriental art, whereas that is an area where Capon – who, incidentally, is an accomplished Oriental linguist – is an expert, and which has had a whole section of the Gallery devoted to it. Today, the word of the director of the Gallery really matters. It was not always thus.

Personally, he is charming, witty and amusing; gregarious; and with exactly that degree of English impishness which appeals to the natural larrikinism of Australians. His wife, Joanna, is an expert in early Australian pressed-metal ceilings, and has done great things in promoting art at the Children's Hospital, Westmead.

Amongst the important principles he has espoused are: (a) always remain horizontal, (b) never stop smoking Havana cigars, (c) never become a Single Issue Fanatic, and (d) respect his "recreations", one of which is "giraffes".

Terry Clarke

Terence John Osborne Clarke was born on 10 February 1935 in Sydney. He was an only child. His secondary schooling consisted of 5 years at All Saints Bathurst and 5 years at Sydney Church of England Grammar School at North Sydney.

In 1952 he proceeded to Sydney University, where he resided at St. Paul's College.

He got a first class honours degree in Music and topped the year in that subject.

He married Lynne, talented daughter of Sir Russell Drysdale.

Since leaving University he taught mathematics (The International School, Cranbrook), which he abandoned for the theatre. He is, and always has been, the darling of the theatre world. He has produced, directed and acted in dozens of plays. He introduced Australian audiences to Harold Pinter. He knows more about Stravinsky than anybody in Australia.

But he will always be chiefly remembered for his musicals. Indeed, he has been the progenitor of the only Australian musicals ever written which matter artistically: "Flash Jim Vaux" (with Ron Blair, author of "The Christian Brother"), and those with Nick Enright "Variations" (his own favourite), "The Venetian Twins" (my favourite, and the most popular), and "Summer Rain" (perhaps the most ambitious). "The Venetian Twins" seems to me to be a work of pure genius; the Goldoni plot, the merry tunes, the swift-moving, exuberant music, the irreverent lines (like "honi Soit qui pense à Mal" referring to one of Australia's former prime ministers), put it almost into the ranks of good Rossini.

He is charming, witty, punning, well read, gregarious and adored.

He loves rich living.

He is a dedicated Marxist

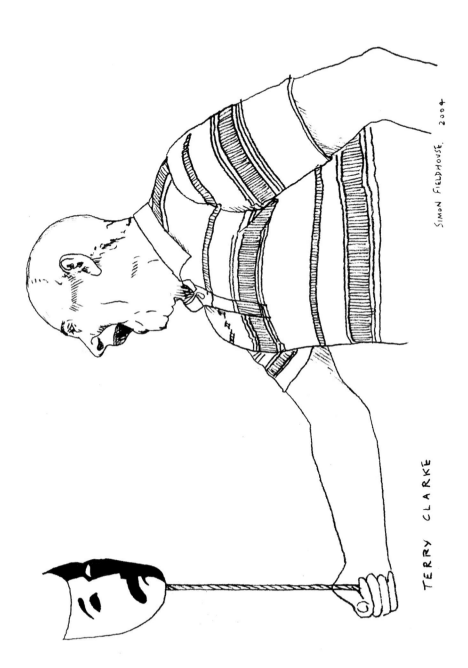

Michael
Connors

I first met Michael Benedict Connors in January - February 1950. I have been a close friend of his in the half century which has elapsed since then. He was then, as he remained for the rest of his life, happy, cheerful, amusing, witty, irreverent, intelligent and well-read. He was also kind and sensitive. To have known him at all was a great blessing, to have know him well for over 50 years was an extraordinary privilege.

We met at the entrance of St John's College, Sydney University. He, born 15th March 1932, was 2 days older than I. He had been educated at the Christian Brothers School at Manly. We studied Arts and Law together. We shared a room in the Right Tower, which, by the time we parted, contained 11 tables, littered with essays, lecture notes, stray publications, empty wine glasses, half filled coffee cups and the dottle of his endless pipes. Whilst appreciative of scholarship, he did not work at his studies with an entirely unremitting fervour.

Considering his cast of mind, it is hardly surprising that he had been from 1944 to 1948, a quiz kid. It suited him, since he knew almost everything that could be known about anything.

If he wanted to, he could have joined the Bar and ended up as a distinguished QC, or alternatively entered into academia and ended up as a famous professor. He did neither, because he considered, and rightly so, that it was more important to devote himself to domestic happiness and leading a decent social life.

ST JOHN'S COLLEGE

MIKE CONNORS

SIMON FIELDHOUSE
2004

He had married, in 1957, the beautiful and aristocratic Mary Candrick. I remember it well because I drove him to the wedding in my motor car which broke down on the way and we were forced to continue our journey by tram. We were all as poor as church mice, and I joined five of his friends in giving him a pop-up toaster to celebrate his nuptials.

He and Mary had dozens of children, and he, with his powerful intelligence could distinguish between them, knowing each one by its name. They, in turn, loved him. I can remember him once saying to me, *"The best way to get friends is to breed them."*

He never paid an active part in politics, although for some years, from 1953 to 1954, he was a follower of Mr B.A. Santamaria, a figure who has in the fullness of time become more important, and more impressive, than people other than Michael Connors realized at the time.

He took a significant part in public life. In 1967 he became a Charter Member of the Rotary Club of Dee Why. From 1973 to 1974 he was President of the Club, and later held various positions. He is a Paul Hanes Fellow.

For many years he was a member of the North Sydney Conference of St Vincent de Paul.

Although from 1958 onwards he attended every day to his work as a solicitor on one of those Northern Beaches of Sydney, he also found time for other professional work, and by giving his services to the Law Society of New South Wales bestowed a modicum of distinction on that grubby body. For many years he was on one of its Legal Aid Review Committees.

But his chief interest outside his family was undoubtedly St John's College. He was a student there for about 6 years and in 1974 was elected a Fellow. In the course of its recent tumultuous years he became its Rector for a while. What, I think, appealed to him about the place was the colour, the fine buildings, the tradition, the whiff of scholarship, the camaraderie and the absence of partisanship or self-interest. Mary also worked tirelessly for the College.

When I look back on his life, there are three things which jump out. The first is his learning. It is nearly impossible to describe just how learned he was in so many fields. To have a conversation with him was an education in itself. You came away more informed, exuberant and sorted out. In the last few weeks of his life, I discussed with him the foreign policy of the Kingdom of the Two Sicilies 1810 – 1820; the rival merits of Chesterton and Belloc; the importance of the elevation of Archbishop Pell to the Cardinalate. He also took time off to explain to me that Menai is not the same suburb as Arncliffe. On one of these occasions, tempted by a private whim, he gave me a football jumper.

The second thing was his great wit. He was one of the most amusing men I have ever met, although in such a spontaneous way that it is now difficult to recall any of his brilliant aphorisms. Recently he was in convulsions of laughter at the thought that the 50,000 Australian sheep floating around the world's oceans might be dumped in New Zealand as war brides.

The third, and most important, thing was his devotion to his religion. He did not merely believe in the Faith, not only practise it, was not only devout; but the Faith was actually part of his very fabric.

And now choirs of angels will sing his beautiful soul to its eternal rest.

Ross
Edwards

Ross Edwards, the composer, was born in Sydney in December 1943, and from a very early age was always interested in music, although in a singularly unsystematic way. In fact, all his early life seemed to be a succession of fits and starts. In 1963 he enrolled in a Bachelor of Arts degree at the University of Sydney, but abandoned it the following year. In 1966 he commenced a Bachelor of Music degree at the University of Adelaide. He took his degree, and later still obtained a Master of Music degree. From then on he became busy either writing or performing music.

Several influences have been detected in his work. One is his attachment to the modern European composers. Roger Covell mocked his mastery of "the fashionable 'tricks' of the *avant-garde*". A second influence is Oriental music, which he developed with his master and friend, Peter Sculthorpe. A third is the music of the Australian bush, of which he became enamoured when he retired for some years to Pearl Beach: this led to his so-called "sacred style".

But a fourth, and far more potent, influence is his development of the Maninya style, characterised by "an abstraction of insect and bird sounds, living tempos and rhythm, angular pentatonic melodies and simple drone-like harmonies". (Nina Appollonov). This was put to spectacular use in the violin concerto of 1988,

ROSS EDWARDS

SIMON FIELDHOUSE 2004

a work which was commissioned by the Australian Broadcasting Commission to celebrate the nation's bicentenary. It was first performed in the Sydney Opera House in August of that year, with Dean Olding as soloist. It has three movements, the first and third being in the Maninya style, and the second being a quiet, soft, serene Intermezzo. The total effect is of a driven, intensely ecstatic work, equal to the violin concerto of William Walton, worthy of comparison with the violin concerti of Shostakovich, and approaching the famous violin concerto of Sibelius. It is clearly a masterpiece, and possibly the only real masterpiece any Australian composer has produced. Other potential rivals look a little thin (like Peter Sculthorpe) or non-existent (like Anne Boyd).

More Please.

Mary
Gaudron

MARY GAUDRON

SIMON FIELDHOUSE

Simon
Fieldhouse

He was born on 25 March 1956. He was educated at Geelong Grammar School and the University of Sydney.

His father, Carnegie Fieldhouse, is a well-known "boutique" solicitor, i.e. a solicitor who will only work for the immensely rich. He, in his time, acquired the famous rural property *Invergowrie* at Exeter, New South Wales. He had five children, of whom Simon is one. The others are depressingly responsible.

Simon dabbled in Arts and Law. Perhaps characteristically, he studied everything but what he should have. By rights, he should have entered the Faculty of Architecture. He did not; but the loss is the Faculty's, not his.

He has an outstanding knowledge of architecture, both instinctive and learned.

He discarded the trappings of rural wealth and devoted himself to architectural draughtsmanship. He went to the office of Messrs Rice and Daubney for two years (1989-1990) and created models for architectural buildings. He then left, and spent his time drawing buildings, trains, ferries, university processions, legal occasions and other national events. In the tradition of Osbert Lancaster and George Molnar, he has given birth to hundreds of architectural drawings of great wit. The production continues. He has become almost morbidly fashionable.

The present book is his first extended exercise in portraiture.

He adores Sophia Loren and Mick Jagger. A worry, this.

He lives with his pretty young mistress in a flat at Darling Point.

SIMON FIELDHOUSE 2004

Robin
Gibson

There are only three of the important, established, well-known private art galleries left in Sydney: Robin Gibson, Rex Irwin and Frank Watters. The greatest of all the private galleries, the Macquarie Galleries, was driven into insolvency and closure by its pretty director, Eileen Chanin. Barry Stern's gallery is still limping on, but at a low level. Rex Irwin sells fashionable foreign artists at enormous prices; and Frank Watters sells mounds of earth and dirty football boots to the chattering classes (he is in training for the Turner Prize). Robin Gibson sells good art to discriminating purchasers. He never seeks to boost sales by exhibiting poor art. Some of his trade competitors do, putting on displays of Bob Dickerson, or even David Boyd.

He was one of a family of six children, born at Ipswich in 1943. He left Queensland in 1963 and worked in the David Jones Art Gallery under the legendary Robert Haines until 1968, when he took a job with the Bonython Gallery in Paddington. When that gallery closed in 1976 he opened his own gallery in Gurner Street in a pretty little terrace house, which he abandoned in 1982 to purchase a much grander affair, a four story building at 278 Liverpool Street Darlinghurst where he established his present gallery, which has been flourishing on that spot ever since. It was built in about 1850 as the town residence

ROBIN GIBSON

SIMON FIELDHOUSE
2003

non lucendo principle, as amongst the ancient Greeks the Furies were called the "Kindly Ones". Even bereavement counsellors look cheerier.

He could be said to be a basically conservative lawyer, although in some respects he is prepared to be "innovative". For example, he seems to welcome the birth of the new right of Privacy.

He is a brilliant, and original, thinker, and it is earnestly to be hoped that his speeches will be collected and published. Mercifully, they lack the unction which so characterised the utterances of his predecessor, Sir Gerard Brennan, and the self-conscious avant-gardism of Sir Anthony Mason. He never utters an unnecessary word.

He has written nothing outside his professional work.

He takes no interest in either music or art.

He does, however, like flowers. He stares at them to make them wilt.

MURRAY GLEESON
CHIEF JUSTICE OF AUSTRALIA

SIMON FIELDHOUSE
2004

Ken
Handley

Mr Justice Kenneth Robert Handley, generally known as "the Saint", is now a senior member of the New South Wales Court of Appeal, after a long and distinguished career as a leader of the New South Wales Bar. He has published major works on *Res Judicata* and *Actionable Misrepresentation*. He loves Fiji, where he feels at home.

Even a year spent as tipstaff to that judicial dullard Mr Justice MacFarlan did not obliterate Handley's famous knowledge of black-letter law.

All his colleagues are worried about him as he looks daily whiter and whiter, thinner and thinner, leaner and leaner. What, they ask themselves, is wrong? The answer is sanctity. He was the Advocate of the (Anglican) Diocese of Sydney from 1970 to 1980, and has been Chancellor of that Diocese since 1980. As well, he has been a member of the Appellate Tribunal of the Anglican Church of Australia since 1980. He loves prayer meetings. At any time of the day or night you can hear him flinging himself on his prayer mat in God-bothering frenzy. His sanctity expands diurnally.

One is reminded of George Eliot's meditations on the Rev. Mr Tryan:

> *"On some ground or other, which his friends found difficult to explain to themselves, Mr Tryan seemed bent on wearing himself out. His enemies were at no loss to account for such a*

JUSTICE KENNETH ROBERT HANDLEY AO

SIMON FIELDHOUSE
2004

course. The Evangelical Curate's sanctity was clearly of too
bad a kind to exhibit itself after the ordinary manner of a
sound, respectable sanctity."

And so the heavenwards imprecations continued.

One of the unfortunate consequences of this spiritual activity
was that Ken has begun to lose, certainly, his subtlety and
perhaps his sense of humour as well. I can remember on one
occasion Sir Gerard Brennan recollecting that, in his younger
days, an old lag said to the Magistrate who sentenced him to a
fortnight's gaol: "You have a face like a Mongolian racing duck's.
And may your dunny burn down." Ken said to his Honour: "Oh
no, Chief Justice, you must have got it wrong, he couldn't have
said that because there is no logical connection between the two
sentences."

He is culturally illiterate. However, his wife is not. She owns
Picassos, Braques, Monets, Marie Laurencins. His eldest son
David is almost single-handedly responsible for the renaissance
in Sydney in the 1990's of sculpture. Another son is married to
the painter Corinne Handley.

J D Heydon

On 14 February 2000 Mr John Dyson Heydon was sworn in as a Judge of the Supreme Court of New South Wales and a Judge of Appeal.

He was a son of the distinguished diplomatist Sir Peter Heydon. He was born in a fashionable house on Leninsky Prospekt in Moscow. He was educated at Sydney Church of England Grammar School. He thence proceeded to the University of Sydney and in 1964 was awarded a Bachelor of Arts (with First Class Honours) and the University Medal in History. Awarded a Rhodes Scholarship, he went to Oxford and did a BA (Jurisprudence) degree, in which in 1966 he took the top first-class honours and was awarded the Martin Wronker prize. He then undertook a BCL course, in which he received the highest first class Honours. He also was awarded the Vinerian Scholarship.

This accomplished, he immediately embarked on an academic career, in which he excelled as brilliantly as he had in his student career. He was a Fellow of, and Tutor at, Keble College at Oxford from 1967 to 1973. He also lectured in evidence and trusts at the Inns of Court School in London from 1969 to 1972, where his distinguished students included the present Mr Justice Gray from the Federal Court of Australia. In 1969 he was a visiting lecturer at the University of Ghana, where he befriended the genial Dr Nkrumah.

He then wrote a series of books, all of which have gained high academic and judicial esteem. The first was *Restraint of Trade Doctrine* in 1971, which was referred to approvingly by the English Court of Appeal at least three times within the next five years. The second was *Economic Torts* in 1973, which sold out almost as soon as it was published. In his preface to the second edition, which was published in 1978, he drew attention to a comment made by some bedint person that "the treatment was difficult to understand", responding politely "there cannot be any account of an economic tort which is comprehensible without effort." In addition to being masterly statements of the law, both books are splendid examples of English prose.

These books were followed by a steady stream of books and articles on Equity, Evidence, Commercial Law, Company Law and Restrictive Practices.

In 1973 he was appointed Professor of Law at the University of Sydney Law School. In 1978 he was made Dean of the Law School, in the days when it was thought that only the most eminent lawyers should hold that position. *Tempora mutantur.*

In 1981 he came to the Bar, and established chambers on Eighth Floor Selborne, then as now the most distinguished set of chambers in Sydney. From his first day at the Bar he enjoyed an enormous practice, and in 1987 took silk.

He was a member of the Bar Council from 1981 to 1986.

He edited the New South Wales Law Reports, the Federal Law Reports, the Australian Bar Review, and probably many more journals and reports.

When Gaudron J retired from the High Court, he was appointed to fill the vacancy. Just as well: otherwise we might have been saddled with a woman, or (even worse) a South Australian.

He is well-liked, amiable, charming, extraordinarily well-read (in non-legal fields as well as in law) and very amusing.

His politics are left-wing, but this went unremarked by the Press until his most recent appointment.

He has substantial pastoral interests, a huge cellar, and a vast art collection (including more than 200 Jean Appletons).

It is said that he likes sport.

DYSON HEYDON

SIMON FIELDHOUSE
2003

J W Howard

John Winston Howard was born in Sydney in about 1960. He immediately escaped from his cot and joined the Liberal Party, in no time becoming Malcolm Fraser's Treasurer, the "Bubba Howard" immortalized by Pickering.

Working with Malcolm Fraser must have been hell. Fraser will go down in history as one of the worst prime ministers Australia has ever had. He was a fraud: a socialist pretending to be a conservative, a centralist pretending to be a states-righter, a proponent of high taxation pretending to be anti-tax, a stupid man pretending to be intelligent (Oxford knew what it was doing when it awarded him a third-class honours degree), and a weak man pretending to be strong. Fraser had but one virtue: he got rid of E. G. Whitlam.

There is this peculiarity about Howard's occupation of the Treasury: he, no doubt under the pressure of his leader, followed a basically socialist line. It was not until the Labour Party gained power and Keating became Treasurer that the Australian dollar was floated, the banking system deregulated, and Liberal Party principles vindicated.

After many vicissitudes he became Prime Minister of Australia in 1996, and at the time of writing (2004) he is still there. Perhaps he will be re-elected at the next election.

He has many triumphs to be celebrated, but undoubtedly his chief one is the management of the economy. During his term of office, budget estimates have been met and actually exceeded, and produced surpluses; balance of payments has improved slightly; unemployment has decreased dramatically (18% under

JOHN HOWARD

SIMON FIELDHOUSE
2004

Whitlam, 10% under Keating, 6% under Howard); the Reserve
Bank interest rate has sunk lower and lower; exports have
increased; taxation has been reduced; the inflation rate has been
contained at about 3% (having soared as high as 20% or more
under Whitlam). All seems well, and people are pleased.

Well, not all people. Howard has managed to make himself
hated by the chatterers, all the chatterers. The list of his enemies
would seem to include university academics, the journalists,
trade unionists, gay and lesbian associations, the Labour Party,
Fr. Frank Brennan SJ, the Anglican Primate of Australia, the
Republican movement, the Democrats, the Greens, the ABC,
Miss Eva Cox, a sprinkling of aborigines and ethnics and Sir
William Deane. Why? There is a simple answer: he has always
been right, and one cannot commit a greater sin. He favoured a
monarchy over a republic, and a majority of Australians agreed
with him. He believed that immigration into Australia should
not be unlimited, and that no illegal immigrants, apart from
genuine refugees, should be admitted: that upset the do-gooders
no end, but the people by their votes showed that they agreed
with him.

I must say that he has another feature which I think appeals
to a majority of people: he is a gentleman. This quality can
be observed when contrasted with the behaviour of Mr Mark
Latham, the current Labour leader. That gentleman saw fit to
call Miss Janet Albrechtsen a "skanky ho" – a phrase which,
apparently (because it is not known to Eric Partridge), means
a "smelly whore". He has not apologized to her since. Now,
put to one side the fact that Miss Albrechtsen is one of the best
political journalists in Australia; the fact is she is a woman, and
one does not speak like that to women. It is also a convenient
measure of the hypocrisy of Mr Howard's chattering opponents
– none of them protested. Yet if Mr Howard had uttered a
similar remark about some left-wing woman journalist (Miss
Eva Cox, for example), the entire sisterhood and every possible
association of journalists would be dancing with indignation like
semi-tormented dervishes.) John Howard does not speak like
that, and has never done so. One reason why he is so popular is
that Australians like good manners.

Michael
Kirby

Michael Donald Kirby was born on 18 March 1939 and educated at Fort Street High School (then, as now, an institution of considerable intellectual distinction), and at the University of Sydney, where he took (simultaneously) degrees in Arts, Law and Economics. He went to the New South Wales Bar, and subsequently became President of the New South Wales Court of Appeal, which position he filled from 1984 to 1996. In 1996 he was appointed to the High Court of Australia, where he still is.

He has held numerous offices and posts, sat on a vast number of committees and tribunals, and conducted (either alone or in company) an untold number of enquiries. This habit began when he was a student, when he was President of the Sydney University ALP Club (a fact which he has suppressed from his lengthy entry in *Who's Who*).

He was a personal advisor to Mr E G Whitlam in the evil days of 1972 to 1975.

Unlike most ALP supporters, he is a fanatical devotee of the monarchy. (Only one ALP member of any Australian parliament preferred the monarchy to a republic in the famous referendum).

Not only of the monarchy, but of all traditional English things –
when sitting on the New South Wales Court of Appeal, he used
to get very cross with any ethnic plaintiff who did not display
enough "stiff upper lip" when enduring his tribulations. It was
on this issue that I was once induced to deplore his "xenophobic
rodomontades". He would love to be a member of the House of
Lords, if only it existed.

His socialist principles have not induced him to distribute
his personal wealth amongst the more deprived members of the
community. He luxuriates in an enormous Sydney waterside
house, outside which poverty-stricken inhabitants of Vaucluse
are living on the footpath.

He loves making speeches. It does not, seemingly, matter to
whom. He will address any conference, association, eisteddfod,
congregation, reunion, symposium, levee or dining club. Nor
does it matter on what subject. He will speak on any aspect of
the law, on modern medicine, on dental decay, on child welfare,
on the activities of UNESCO, on the Arab-Jew problem, on
music, on economics, on the Stock Exchange, and on the multiple
complications of the computer. Recently he spoke to the Loya
Jirga at Kabul on "The Message of Islam" and to a gathering of
senior monks at Phnom-Penh on "The Necessity for Silence".

Despite the almost innumerable number of things he says on a
multitude of occasions, there is almost nothing he has said which
I can remember. One thing only that I can think of: that Dr Evatt
was a champion of civil rights. And that utterance is totally false.
When did Dr Evatt ever denounce the Soviet Gulag?

A curious subject which has absorbed much of his time
and attention is breast-feeding. I cannot remember his point
of view. Perhaps it is that the habit infringes the child's civil
rights; perhaps it is that breast-feeding is the modern woman's
ultimate achievement. At any rate, whatever his point of view,
he espouses it with a rare fervour. Once he was invited to talk
about it at a gathering of African chiefs, and it was only when he
mounted the rostrum on which sat his principal hosts with their
plumages unruffled and nose-bones polished, that he realised the
subject he was supposed to speak on was not "Breast Feeding"
but "Press Freedom".

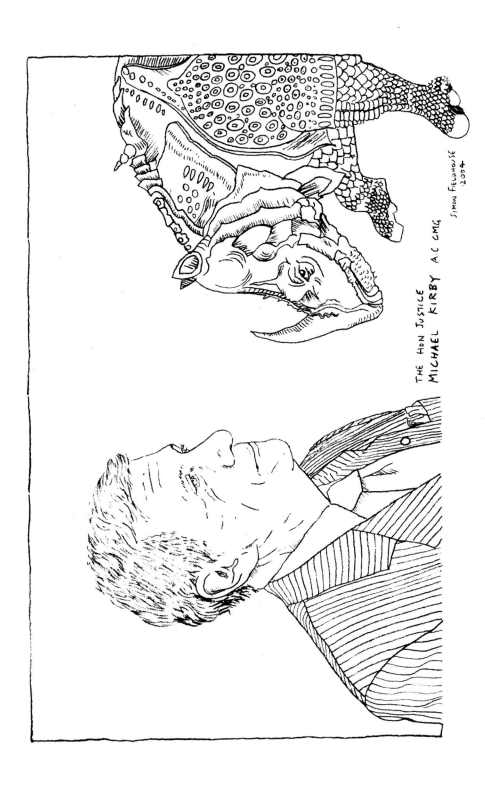

THE HON JUSTICE
MICHAEL KIRBY A.C CMG

SIMON FIELDHOUSE
2004

His legal philosophy may, I think, be summarized as follows: (1) When a superior appellate court changes the law (which it obviously does from time to time), it is exercising a power which on a correct legal analysis can only be described as legislative, and (2) therefore, the Court, being seized of legislative power, should exercise it whenever and wherever it wants to, as if it were Parliament, and that, irrespective of principle and precedent. The non sequitur involved in the second proposition is fairly obvious.

He has no knowledge of art whatever, and yet, curiously, he is an excellent draughtsman. He constantly exercises this faculty whilst he is sitting on a case. I once had a large portfolio of the drawings he made in Court, but some person from Porlock has stolen it.

His long time partner, Johan van Vloten, is a charming and intelligent Dutchman, full of learning about his home country.

He is a person of great generosity and kindness, and I have benefited from it.

Lou
Klepac

Lou Klepac was born in 1936, although he looks much older, in Croatia (and not, as some people seem to think in Serbia, or some even worse place). He was educated in various academies in Venice and Trieste, at the Modern School in Perth (an oxymoron if ever there was one), and at the University of Western Australia.

He married his present wife, the charming Brenda, in 1961. He has suppressed all reference to that event in his widely-circulated Curriculum Vitae.

He has made two contributions to Australian life. The first is in the area of art gallery management. From 1964 to 1966 he was the Curator of Paintings at the Art Gallery of Western Australia, and the (curiously titled) Keeper of Paintings at the Art Gallery of South Australia from 1966 to 1970. He then became the Deputy Director of the Art Gallery of Western Australia. In all these positions he tried, with some success, to introduce twentieth century art into Australia, an endeavour which provoked the wrath of the Country Party grandees of Western Australia.

The second is publishing. He has produced book after book, usually on people who matter (for example, Lloyd Rees and David Strahan) but sometimes on people who matter not at all (for example, Louis Kahan and Shay Docking). They are, invariably, well-produced, with the illustrations true, and the text not inane; what is more, they always come at an affordable price.

He is gregarious, and gossips amusingly and endlessly. He is a scandalmonger.

Simon Fieldhouse 2004

Lou Klepac

Dame Leonie
Kramer

Dame Leonie Kramer is the most distinguished woman in Australia. Born in October 1924, she was educated at Melbourne and Oxford Universities. Since then, she has been prominent as an author, academic, public servant, lecturer and business woman. It would be tedious to list the long list of positions she has held with such *réclame*: they fill a column or two of *Who's Who*.

She is almost universally admired. I say "almost" because there are one or two disgruntled chatterers who would demur. Patrick White was one. He made a famously vicious remark about her in his autobiography, *Flaws in the Glass*. Of that remark two things may be said: first, it was not original – it was a loutishly expressed version of a famous couplet by Alexander Pope about Hervey ("Sporus"); secondly, she has never responded, not being vindictive.

The nineteen forties and fifties were Australia's most prominent period of great poetry. It was the period of A.D. Hope, James McAuley, David Campbell, Gwen Harwood and Judith Wright. It was typical of Dame Leonie that she was a close personal friend of all these poets, and wrote most beautifully about them.

DAME LEONIE KRAMER

SIMON FIELDHOUSE
2004

If ever there was a group of writers who were blessed with a tough, intellectual cast of mind beneath a light lyric grace, this was it.

It was not only poets she espoused. She also wrote some important work on Henry Handel Richardson and Martin Boyd, who paid her a heartfelt compliment in his autobiography.

Her Grosvenor Gallery work with poets and novelists did not occupy the whole of her attention. She devoted some time to the directorships of large mining and banking companies.

One coterie amongst whom enthusiasm about Dame Leonie is muted is the Feminist Movement. Dame Leonie is one of those prominent women who gain no praise from the Feminists: others are Lady Thatcher, once Prime Minister of Great Britain; Lady Donaldson, once Lord Mayor of London; the late Duchess of Norfolk, once Lord Lieutenant of the County of West Sussex; and Mother Teresa, the poor Albanian nun who devoted herself to the poor of Calcutta. These people are snarled at, not admired. Instead, the Feminists worship scarcely couth viragos like Germaine Greer. One can hear them humming little tunes about the necessity of never shaving their legs.

In fact, the animosity of this group mounted steadily when Dame Leonie was Chancellor of the University of Sydney. They allied themselves with ignorant students, second-grade academics, rebel left-wingers, ambitious office-holders and plain fruitcakes. Indeed, if one views her enemies in Senate, one can hardly enthuse about their quality. Yet they toppled her. It was like Acteon being devoured by his own mongrels.

John
Lehane

On 11 September 2001 John Robert Felix Lehane died, an enormous loss to the legal profession.

He was born on 18 October 1941 in Sydney, the son of Felix Lehane and his wife Jessie (née Vicars), whose sister is Lady Windeyer, Sir Victor's widow. He was educated at Sydney Grammar School, and at the University of Sydney, from which he graduated BA with first class Honours in Latin (1964), LLB with first class honours and the University Medal (1969) and LLM with first class honours (1980). He resided at St. Paul's College.

He served articles of clerkship in 1966 with Messrs Allen Allen & Hemsley solicitors of Sydney. He was admitted as a solicitor on 14 March 1969. He then worked for 2 years as an employed solicitor, until in 1971 he became a member of the firm. He stayed there until October 1995, being Managing Partner (1990-1993) and Chairman of Partners (1994-5). In October 1995 he was appointed by the Keating Government as a Judge of the Federal Court of Australia – arguably the only good decision that Government ever made. Although he had almost never seen the inside of a Court, and knew nothing of practice and procedure and very little of the law of evidence, he was a triumphant success as a judge.

He was a lecturer in Equity at the University of Sydney Law School. He published many articles and studies on various aspects of equity and commercial law, in which he had formidable expertise. He was one of the authors of Meagher Gummow & Lehane *Equity: Doctrines and Remedies*, the leading Australian text book in that field. Anyone who reads the chapter in that book dealing with equitable assignments, or the chapter on receivers, will at once appreciate his unique combination of profound learning, precise thinking and verbal elegance.

His learning was profound: in the Bible, in Greek and Latin, in English literature, and in law. And from that learning he honed the skills of precise thinking and precise writing. To read the observations which accompanied any belief which he sent you was a delight: his analytical formulation of whatever question he was nominally asking you both outlined a problem which had previously escaped your attention and also enabled you to solve it.

His precision of thought enabled him to draft enormously complex documents like mining joint venture agreements and leveraged loans of aircraft. When he committed pen to paper each word had its own precise and accurate meaning, no superficiality or inexactitude being tolerated; and this was so even when his prose was at its most Jamesian. When a student he was awarded ten marks out of ten for an examination answer consisting of no more than six lines.

He was extraordinarily modest, with nothing to be modest about.

He should have been appointed to the High Court.

To say all that, however, might suggest a rather more severe person than he actually was. He had a grand, but concealed and impish, sense of humour. I cannot remember any Voltairean epigrams or Wildean paradoxes bursting from his lips, but I distinctly do remember him often exploding with laughter. He was intrigued by the wording of an easement in South Australia

JOHN LEHANE

which was expressed to last for "a term of perpetuity less one day"; he was delighted when I showed him a will in which a testatrix (inevitably a testatrix) left her residuary estate "to all the people in Australia, or failing that to their children." In the first edition of Meagher, Gummow & Lehane it was said of s98 of the amended *Common Law Procedure* Act that "Myers J had no hand in begetting it", and John became convulsed with laughter when Glass JA observed that the sentence betrayed an elementary ignorance of biology.

Constant Lambert, in his book *Music Ho*, said that if you tried to describe Richard Strauss's music you would stress the brilliance of his orchestration, if it was Sibelius you would stress the austerity of his bleak Nordic melodies, but if it was Mozart all you could say was, accurately but dully, that his music was wonderful. In a way, one has a similar problem talking of John Lehane. He did not utter any famous statements, he never got violently angry, he never got drunk, he did nothing outrageous, he was not colourful yet he was one of the greatest lawyers and one of the nicest men any of us will ever meet. He had great fastidiousness and was one of those rare people, sincere and unostentatious, to whom the conduct of life was *ars artium*.

Janet
McCredie

Janet McCredie was born about 70 years ago, the daughter of two doctors – her father a gynaecologist and her mother a radiologist.

Her secondary education was at Ascham, Darling Point, a school then (and since) notable for the excellence of its academic standards. She shone in scientific subjects and did brilliantly in the Leaving Certificate (although, manifestly, her knowledge of history is sadly deficient and her knowledge of Greek and Latin non-existent). She then went to the Women's College at the University of Sydney, where she studied Medicine, and graduated with an Honours degree. She has done much post-graduate work both in Sydney and in London.

She then returned to Sydney and settled down to practising radiology in her mother's business at Campsie. She did this for some years. Her work was so highly esteemed that she was eventually made Professor of Radiology at the University of Sydney, a chair specially invented for her.

It was during her work at Campsie that she made her most famous discovery, i.e. that the drug Thalidomide causes birth defects in babies by its operation on the nervous system of the embryo. It was an important scientific discovery, and earned her a M.D from the University of Sydney and an AO from the Queen. It also earned her a controversy with a notorious doctor.

He had borrowed her work, declined to return it to her, and publicly claimed it as his own. He also knew so little about the subject that before he stole her work he claimed that the drug worked its mischief by deforming the bone structure (not the nerves) of the foetus (not the embryo).

She has busied herself with the affairs of the Women's College, and has been the Chairman (which she calls "the Chair"!) of its council for two decades – far too long for its good, or her own.

She has built up a healthy art collection. She had a head start, as her mother was a very good painter. Many of her aunts (of whom she had a great number) left their estates to her in their wills, by which stroke of fortune she has accumulated a ridiculously large number of oil paintings by Lloyd Rees, as well as much real estate. (All in all, she is absurdly rich.) However, her knowledge of art is as deficient as her knowledge of history. She cannot distinguish an Augustus John from a Gwen John, and confuses Ben Nicolson with Ben Nicholson.

And there is a darker side to her: she loves Mendelssohn, she votes Labour, and she puts milk in her scrambled eggs.

She is not married, but

JANET MᶜCREDIE

SIMON FIELDHOUSE 2004

Roddy **Meagher**

I am the second son of Peter James Meagher and his wife Marian Beatrice. I was born at a small town in New South Wales called Temora, which I regard with as much affection as Hesiod did Askra. The date was 17 March 1932, although the event was not registered until 1957.

My father had two outstanding characteristics. One was that he was the best looking man in the world. In fact, the main reason why I developed an early inferiority complex was that I could not stand everyone to whom I, a conspicuously plain child, was introduced saying "He hasn't got his father's looks". A glance at his epigoni would discover no hint of beauty. The other was that he was the nicest man in the world.

My mother was always in a continual depression, caused by contemplating the fact that she was related to Patrick White.

Since there are thousands of Meaghers in New South Wales, I might indicate which ones are my siblings. My elder brother, Peter, has three brilliant daughters: one is a banker in the United States of America, one is the senior nurse in a big Sydney hospital, and one is a painter and print-maker. My brother Christopher is an ex-bullfighter and ex-solicitor, who has three passions in life: keeping silent, gambling and playing golf, the last of which has landed him in hospital on three occasions for heart transplants. My sister is married into the English army and lives at Earls Colne, a charming village in the northern reaches of Essex. My youngest brother Philip, lives at Bankstown (a suburb of Sydney), has 20 children, and is obscenely rich. One of his

MR JUSTICE RODERICK PITT MEAGHER

SIMON FIELDHOUSE
2004

children, a boy called Wayne Julian, is an excellent artist. In
his day, Philip, who seems more dim than dashing, was pursued
by Christine Keeler, Princess Michael, Clover Moore and René
Rivkin. The fabulously beautiful Miss Amy Meagher (now
Gerstl), who lives in the Collaroy – Cronulla district, is not a
sibling; she is my beloved daughter. No other Meaghers matter.

At the age of nine I was sent to boarding school at Riverview,
then in truth, now nominally, a Jesuit institution. In those days
the ranks of teachers included Fr. Daniel O'Connell, probably
the greatest astronomer in Australia; Fr. Bourke-Gaffney, a geo-
physicist; Fr. Austin Ryan, the best Classics master in the State;
and Fr Frank Dennett, an excellent historian and litterateur.
The role of the Jesuits was constituted by obedience to the Holy
See and the promotion of scholarship. The former has now
been abandoned in favour of Liberation Theology. The latter
has bowed to the pressure of Social Purpose Studies and the
provision of soup kitchens for the poor. In my days Fr. Ryan
taught us all the Greek classics, whereas Sydney Grammar
School taught no Greek. Nowadays Riverview is abandoning
Greek, but Grammar has a flourishing Greek class and has
introduced Sanskrit into its syllabus. I have seen the handful of
Jesuits left at Riverview, dressed in hippie attire, dancing round
a barbeque singing "the Internationale". Fr. Frank Brennan is
the archetype of the modern Jesuit: short on Greek verbs, long
on witchetty grubs.

Thence I went to St John's College at the University of
Sydney, and studied Arts and Law. After graduation I practised
at the Bar of New South Wales, not brilliantly but *haud sine
gloria*. In 1989 I went to the Court of Appeal.

My politics are left-wing, but in a very balanced way. I think
I might inch a little to the right.

The one good thing I have done in my professional life was
(with the cooperation of two colleagues) write a book on Equity.

Penny Meagher

Penny Meagher - or, more accurately, Elma Penelope Meagher-was born on 22 April 1935. She was the elder daughter of Keith Moss, a publisher, and his wife, the charming and intelligent Nell Cohen, only daughter of Sir Samuel Cohen.

She died on 5 June 1995, aged just sixty.

She and I were married on 3 July 1962, and she gave me over 30 years of unalloyed bliss. We had one child, Amy.

She was educated at Ascham School, Darling Point, and (if one uses the verb in its loosest sense) at Frensham, Mittagong. She then went to the University of Sydney, where she studied (of all things) Economics. Noting that she had neither knowledge of, nor interest in, that subject I once asked her why she had studied it, only to receive the reply "I thought it might do some good for the poor little black babies in Africa". She thus displayed, from earliest years, not only a caring temperament but also a striking mastery of feminine logic.

A little book has been published to record her achievement in painting and drawing.

Her talent in both was considerable. It was not inherited from either parent, although her mother had a passing interest in art. Her father was profoundly ignorant of the subject, to his own satisfaction.

She, apparently, did drawings from a very early age. In 1952, on a trip to London, she enrolled at the Chelsea School of Art and spent some months there. Later, in about 1960-1962, she did a course at the East Sydney Technical College; and, later still, another graduate course at the University of New South Wales. For a few years in the late sixties, she was a director of the Macquarie Galleries. All the while she drew and painted, towards the end of her life at a little cottage at Darlington which she used as her own studio, and also permitted other artists to use.

While she worked continuously (in the sense that at no time did she take a long break from work), she spent comparatively little of her days at her easel. She was easily diverted by domestic tasks.

Yet, in retrospect, the work she left behind is considerable in bulk and of an extraordinarily high standard.

She never had a one-man show, although she was about to do so when she contracted the leukaemia which struck her down. She did, however, exhibit on a few occasions in group shows, including an important show of Still Lifes at David Jones Art Gallery in November- December 1984. In each such group show she sold every painting she exhibited.

She was, by nature, very sympathetic and tender. She was the gentlest person I have ever met.

Her art reflects this gentleness, catching all the of the nuances of her universe, be it her houses, her rooms, her furniture or her flowers. She poured into her canvases all her empathy and feeling. This will be evident to anyone who glances at her work. But such a person will also note that her gentleness never degenerates into weakness. He will also note her delight in colour (she rarely used black or brown), her able draftsmanship, and her generosity of feeling.

Like other women painters (eg Margaret Preston) she could produce works which can be fairly described as strong.

She almost never painted abstract paintings: that was not her ticket. Nor, except when she was a student, did she do genre paintings. Her paintings were always on the small side. She rarely did landscapes. She did do some, but not many, portraits. She detested la grande machine. Post-modernism did not enthuse her. Her forte, particularly in later years, was still lifes.

PENNY MEAGHER

SIMON FIELDHOUSE

It is not fortuitous that her two most favourite modern painters were Bonnard and Gwen John. What they had in common was what she herself most excelled in: paintings which exuded the spirit of domestic intimacy.

Her still lifes were not any accidental collections of objects. She placed things carefully, however apparently haphazardly; using fruit, and in particular pears, often placing them engagingly off-centre, for the beauty of their form, for volume and for composition.

She still lives in her art. *Non omnis est mortua*.

Brian
Moore

Brian Moore, who died in June 2003, was born in Katoomba in 1951, but grew up (to the extent that he did grow up) in Manly. In 1971 he joined the David Jones Art Gallery, and from then on worked in fine arts and antiques until he opened his own gallery in November 2000.

Brian was marvellous. Kind, good looking, charming, friendly and amusing. He had none of the aggression or sharp edges one would expect of a gallery director. All his ways were ways of gentleness and all his paths were peace. And he was young. But, in the happy no-time of his sleeping, death took him by the heart.

I should like to stress two of his many qualities. The first is his generosity. When he was running "Kaleidoscope", that Mecca of fine art, he once had a pair of double screens, 17th Century Spanish, leather, painted with foliage and exotic birds. I lusted after them. I asked the price and was told $14,000. That was about 14 times what I could afford. However, I dreamed endlessly of them, and eventually decided to buy them even if I could not pay for them. I thought that, once I got them in my hands, it was his business to get the money, not mine. When I then marched into "Kaleidoscope" and asked for them, Brian said to me: "I am afraid I cannot sell them to you. I sold them to someone else yesterday."

Two years later he rang me up and said that the client who bought the screens had gone bankrupt and that his trustee wanted $4000 for the screens, was I still interested. I was. So

I now own them. But it shows how Brian was able to sell me for $4000 some beautiful objects which he could have sold for a much higher figure. Why? Simply out of generosity.

The other quality is his courage. Although consumed with that awful malady, which a deity whom we are compelled to call benevolent visited on him, he was always cheerful, never complained, ever protested his good health, was planning to come back to the gallery even 3 days before his death.

He never did a common thing or mean. He was a noble essence.

BRIAN MOORE 1951 - 2003   SIMON FIELDHOUSE

Margaret Olley

Everyone feels he knows Margaret Olley. If he has not seen her in real life, he has on television or in the newspapers. The pretty, slightly chubby face; the warm smile; the braided hair, often peeping out from under an absurd home-made hat; the alluring drawl; the general atmosphere of charm tempered by intelligence, taste and shrewdness. We all know that. And to make certain we do, all good artists have drawn or painted that famous face: Dobell, Drysdale, Donald Friend, Jeff Smart, the great Fairweather, Kevin Connor, Judy Cassab - and Margaret Olley. She would be the Grand Old Lady of Australian painting, if only she were old.

Margaret Hannah Olley was born in Lismore in 1923 and hurried off to live in Brisbane, which is in Queensland. The bulk of her life was spent in that Long Weekend between the two wars, when the École de Paris was at its height. And she took to it with ease. By the age of 24 she had graduated from Technical College in both Brisbane and Sydney; she had come to live in Sydney, which is her preferred Australian home; and she had won her first major art prize, the Mosman Art Prize. A year later she had her first one-man show at the Macquarie Galleries. And by this time she was a member of that distinguished group of Sydney painters who dominated Australian painting in the 40's and 50's and who have, thanks to the mischief of Robert Hughes, become subsequently known as "The Charm School".

Since then she has gone from strength to strength. She has had solo exhibitions about every other year in London, Sydney or Brisbane. She has won more than twelve major art prizes, the

M. OLLEY

Simon Fieldhouse

most important of which being probably the Helena Rubinstein Portrait Prize in Western Australia. She is represented in about every major art collection in Australia, but not – horresco referens - in the art collection of the University of Sydney. She has lived in France and there mingled with such important figures as Chagall, Baboulene, Jean Marchand, Sir Francis Rose and Gertrude Stein.

She has excelled in both drawing and painting. She has done many splendid paintings of Australian landscape, particularly of the countryside around Sofala and Hill End. She has a large number of portraits to her credit, including three or four major ones of Margaret Olley. But, above all, she has made a speciality of oil paintings of interiors and still lifes. In this regard she has absorbed the lessons of Cezanne and the École de Paris. Her still lifes are not mere collections of disparate objects, haphazardly arranged. They are deliberate, if seemingly relaxed, arrangements which demonstrate careful construction, a great sense of colour, beautiful modalities, a control of volume, a skilful use of contrasts, a sense of light, and a sensuous delight in beautiful things. She is Australia's answer to Chardin.

During the 1970's she fell momentarily from critical favour for not displaying a social and political conscience, for being uninvolved in feminist, communist and environmental issues. One Canberra critic said that if one looked at one of the beautiful paintings one would not suspect that motor cars were speeding in the streets. In those heady days the National Gallery of Victoria had a major "art" exhibition which did not contain a single painting. She continued as she was, she felt that a painter should paint, and she said to that Canberra critic "tant pis". Today those 1970 views seem absurd, and crowds of art lovers thank Olley on bended knees that she did what she did.

Not, of course, that she has no views on matters of politics. Indeed, she made a major contribution to the recent Republic v Monarchy debate.

She has also done two other things. One is encourage the young. There is hardly an art gallery opening that she does not attend and bless. The other is public philanthropy. Through the medium of her Olley Foundation she has lavished largesse on the Art Gallery of NSW, donating such major works as great Degas drawings.

Dr N A
Packham

Nicholas Anthony Packham was born 72 years ago at Wagga Wagga. He went to many schools, but mainly to Christian Brothers Waverley. He did well at school, because he was frighteningly intelligent. For the same reason, when he went to Sydney University he obtained good degrees in Dentistry, Medicine and Law. Somehow or other he also acquired diplomas in plumbing and theology.

At his peak he was one of the 2 or 3 top surgeons in Sydney.

Susie, his current wife, a pretty little thing, was formerly an actress, as were her three predecessors.

He is a well-known investor in real estate, an activity which has fuelled his appetite for litigation. It is probable that he has, on his desk, a framed photograph of his hero, Katherine Wentworth. Nearly every year he buys another share in the Harbour Bridge. He fills his house with junk.

He plays bridge, but badly.

He is infinitely kind.

He is what the French called toqué. More than somewhat.

DR N.A PACKHAM

Simon Fieldhouse 2004

What a piece of prose! What a riot of incomprehensibility! What does it mean? What exactly is "the theology of communion"? Who is to have dialogue with whom? It is the voice of Vatican Two barking at the door. That suicidal assembly, the chattering classes at prayer, has proved nothing except that if one gives up reading Latin one forgets how to write English. Pat, please note.

Ricky
Ponting

RICKY PONTING

P J
Ryan

Dr P J Ryan, one of Queensland's most prominent medical practitioners, has never been known, in the whole of his 70 years, to utter more than one word, and that is "*Poop*".

Pierre
Ryckmans

According to Mr Justice Spigelman, Pierre Ryckmans is the most outstanding intellectual in Australia. I quite agree. This country should count itself lucky that he has decided to perch here.

His family is an old and distinguished one. All educated Australians will remember that his namesake, and uncle, was Governor-General of the Belgian Congo during the Second World War, and how his deft behaviour in that office prevented the Nazi authorities in Belgium from exploiting the economy of the Congo, a country which in those *beaux jours* was well governed. And most educated Australians will be conscious of the existence of an Old Master, Nicolas Ryckmans, in the seventeenth century, a colleague and follower of Rubens – a *petit maître* to be sure, but still a *maître*.

Pierre himself was born in Brussels, educated at the University of Louvain, and settled in Australia in 1970, after a stint in the Belgian Embassy at Peking, where he learned both Mandarin and Cantonese. He gave the Boyer Lectures in 1996. He is a member of the Royal Belgian Academy, taking Simenon's stall. He was the Professor of Chinese Studies at the University of Sydney 1987-1993. In 1964 he married Chang Hanfang, who is as close to a piece of Dresden china as it is possible to be. He is the father of the beauteous Jeanne Ryckmans, toast of the Archibald Prize competition.

He is a very important writer. I shall endeavour to list some, but not all, of his works. There is a group of books on contemporary China: *The Chairman's New Clothes*, *Chinese*

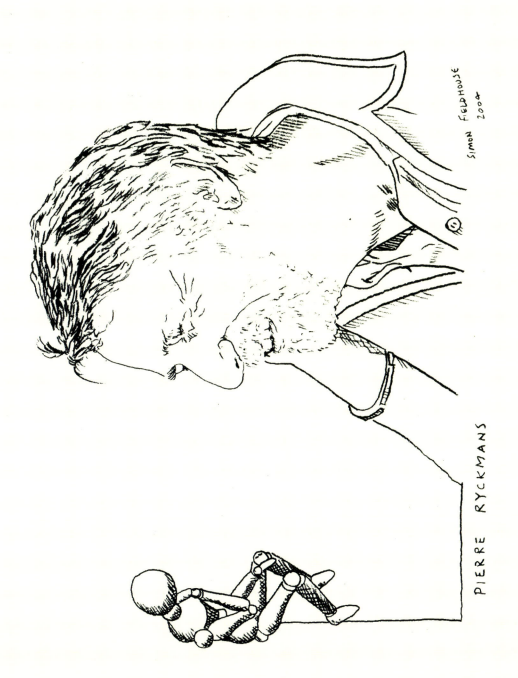

SIMON FIELDHOUSE
2000

PIERRE RYCKMANS

Shadows and *The Burning Forest*.   Perhaps their greatest importance is their demonstration that Mao, then an idol of the liberal left, was a major disaster for his Chinese people and an enemy of civilisation.   Then there is his fiction, of which *The Death of Napoleon* is the most important item.   It is equal to any of Voltaire's *Contes Philosophiques*: a brilliantly written novella with a background of profundity.   It has won major literary prizes in England, the United States, France and Australia.   It will always remain in print.   In the world of art, where both he and his wife are skilled performers, he has written with great illumination of Ian Fairweather; perhaps, one might think, an odd choice, until one remembers their common debt to China. Finally, in this list (and it's not a complete list), one has his much-acclaimed edition of Confucius's *Analects*, said by the experts to be the best translation of that work in existence.

He has an enormously stimulating mind.   He is not suffocated by political correctness.

He dislikes Jean Lacouture, and detests Bernard-Henri Levy. It is, therefore, surprising that he likes both D H Lawrence and Céline.   One earnestly hopes that he has no time for Romain Rolland.

Everyone's attention should be drawn to a significant fact about his career.   When the Senate of the University of Sydney debated his appointment to the Chair of Chinese Studies, Mr E G Whitlam (and his supporters) opposed the appointment – on the ground that it might not be welcome to "our Chinese friends".   It is a fair demonstration of that gentleman's reverence of academic values.   It is as if, in the thirties, one had opposed the appointment of a Jewish scholar to a chair of German on the ground that it would not be welcome to the German Government! (Perhaps, it is in character with other behaviour by Mr Whitlam. He always opposed granting help to the Independent Timor movement, on the ground that it might upset his friends in Jakarta.   It is the language of the Cliveden set. Perhaps he is Sir Samuel Hoare come again.)

G J
Samuels

Born in 1923, Gordon Samuels was educated in England, taking a degree at Oxford when a resident of Balliol, and devoting himself to the study of law when the Second World War was concluded. He spent the war years in the Royal Artillery, emerging as Captain in the 96th (Royal Devon Yeomanry) Field Regiment. In 1948 he was admitted to the Inner Temple. And then, wholly inexplicably, he migrated to Australia, where in 1952 he was admitted to the New South Wales Bar.

From then on, there was no looking back. He was a leading barrister, a Queen's Counsel, a President of the New South Wales Bar Association, and a Judge of the Court of Appeal of the Supreme Court of New South Wales. And in 1957 he married Jacqui Kott from Perth, the well-known actress whom most of us will always remember starring in *Who's Afraid of Virginia Woolf?*

In 1996 he was appointed Governor of New South Wales, a job he fulfilled with maximum distinction.

If one were to choose his most outstanding characteristic, it is undoubtedly – and more so than in the case of any other person discussed in this book – literary style. Tall, good-looking, urbane, invariably well-dressed and well-groomed, with a glorious English voice, he is the very embodiment of "the effortless superiority of the Balliol man". He writes beautifully, and was (and is) one of the very best after-dinner speakers in Australia.

He has always been a great patron of the theatre, the cinema and the art galleries. He was a great Chancellor for many years of the institution now known as the University of New South Wales, which, under his aegis, has surpassed the University of Sydney in many respects. Cliff Pugh has painted a splendid portrait of him in his robes of office.

I should hate it to be thought that he is without sin. He once said I did not know what I was talking about when I blamed Beneš for transferring part of his country to Stalin. He did not, however, explain to me how else Ruthenia became part of the Ukraine.

As a judge, his judgments were, almost invariably, correct; but unlike others, he was usually mellifluous as well as correct. Much that he wrote could go straight into the Oxford Book of English Prose. I refer to but four examples: first, a passage from his judgment in the reported case of *Moorhouse v Angus & Robertson (No 1)*:

> *It will be convenient to deal first with the plaintiff's appeal and the question of abandonment. Upon this topic, we had the benefit of a most interesting and learned argument from both sides. Although it is tempting to resolve the possible conflict of doctrine between Viner (Vin Abr Waife 409) and The Doctor and Student, Selden Society, 1 2 c 5I, p 290, on the one hand, and Blackstone, 17th ed, (1830) Commentaries I, p 295; II p 9, on the other, involving, as it would, consideration of the rights of property in shrouds or coffins (Haynes's case (1614 12 Co Rep 113; 77 ER 1389) and diseased pigs (R v Edwards & Stacey (1877) 13 Cox CC 384), I find it possible, by the exercise of some resolution, to deny myself this indulgence.*

Secondly, a quotation from his unreported judgment in *Newnham v Tarbert*, a *Family Provision Act* case:

> *I agree. The deceased and respondent appear to have lived together in a degree of disorganization or indeed of squalor, distinguished by regular infusions of alcohol, which both of them found entirely congenial. The respondent provided the deceased with companionship and some degree of domestic economy which otherwise he might have found difficult to*

GORDON SAMUELS

Simon Fieldhouse 2004

*obtain, since his physical condition was generally distasteful
and his temperament aggressive and overbearing.*

*I do not agree that conduct, in order to satisfy the formula
concerning contribution to the welfare of the deceased person
within s9(3)(a)(ii) of the Family Provision Act, must
conform to some external objective criterion of virtue and moral
improvement. If that was so then the Act would disentitle, for
example, a female spouse who was a happy sloven with the most
rudimentary notions of housekeeping and who encouraged her
companion to join her in slaking an appetite for alcohol and
cholesterol-rich foods, but whose wit, courage and affection
illuminated his life.*

*It seems to me quite possible in the present case that the
deceased and the respondent were quite happy together and, as
the learned Acting Master pointed out, when she did leave him
for a time, he went after her and persuaded her to return.*

Thirdly, an observation on the married state from the reported
case of *Bryson v Bryant*:

*I do not myself regard this as an hopelessly antique view of
life suitable only to the regulation of a society whose principles
have been substantially abandoned and whose expectations are
in the process of a radical re-appraisal. The term "natural
love and affection" which is used in the cases certainly has a
somewhat old-fashioned and orotund ring about it but it should
be remembered that the preference by some for relationships
untrammelled by any formal ties is produced by the view that
the reality of the relationship will survive without the need
to formalize it. In that respect, of course, it represents the
triumph of natural love and affection.*

Fourthly, an extract from an extra-curial writing:

*Gummow is terrifying his colleagues by slightly increasing
his ordinary work rate. It has been suggested that he might like
to write the parties' submissions as well as the judgment, thus
preserving the unity of style and intellectual standard.*

(It is not easy to see why everyone enjoys mocking little
alopecic Gummow; but, on second thoughts, perhaps it
is.)

Few, indeed, are the Australian Judges who could write like that. Jordan CJ was one, so was Kitto J; so, too, famously, was Rich J (or whoever wrote his judgments). Is there anyone else? Could one imagine Gummow J, or Gaudron J, saying anything with felicity? And, by way of contrast, consider this example of judicial aridity from Mahoney J, as he then was, in the reported case of *A.S.L. Developments Ltd v Sargent*:

> *The cases in which…a person is held by law to have lost the right of rescission sometimes are cases in which the statements of principle are couched in terms appropriate to the exercise of the right ("he must be taken to have elected not to rescind the contract") and sometimes are cases in which the judgments are couched in terms of the giving up of the right ("he must be taken to have waived the right"). Viewed in the abstract, the cases in which the right of rescission has been held to be exercised or given up in the absence of knowledge or intention by the party in question are, it may be, not properly to be put either in the category of exercise or in the category of giving up or waiver, and should be put in a separate category which recognizes that such knowledge and intention as I have referred to are not essential to cases which fall within it.*

And, by way of further example, consider this extract from Priestley JA, in the reported case of *B & B Constructions v Brian A Cheeseman*; part motherly, part soya-beans-and-basic-English:

> *One reason why the particular question of legal theory is difficult is that it is seeking to find an answer, or a set of answers, to cover a variety of different situations … I think the actual practice of the courts shows different criteria being used for the selection of extrinsic material in different types of case.*

More Samuels, please.

J J Spigelman

James Jacob Spigelman, the current Chief Justice of New South Wales, was born in Poland in 1946, and came to Australia in 1949. He was educated at Sydney Boys High School, of which he is a rather more distinguished alumnus than Mr Justice Marcus Einfield. After studying law at the University of Sydney, he went to the Bar and had a career of almost unparalleled distinction there, excelling both in private law and in public law.

He is short (or should one say "vertically challenged"?) and tubby (or should one say "gravitationally challenged"?). He looks like Cyril Connolly.

A perusal of *Who's Who* will testify to the variety and importance of the offices he has held: on the Art Gallery of New South Wales, the Australian Film School, the Law Reform Commission, the Observatory, the Powerhouse and heavens knows what else besides.

A note in the same book states: "Snr. Advisor and Princip. Private Sec to P.M. Australia 1972-1975". This refers to his occupation during the grim years when Mr E.G. Whitlam was Prime Minister. He was one of that man's Kitchen Cabinet, one of the three wunderkinder who were supposed to keep him on the rails (the other two being Michael Kirby and the late Peter Wilenski). One episode which happened in this connection is not generally known: when the vacancy for the position of Governor-General which was filled by Sir John Kerr first arose, Spigelman strongly advised Mr Whitlam to appoint Cardinal Gilroy. That would indeed have led to some curious results.

CHIEF JUSTICE OF NSW
THE HON. JAMES JACOB SPIGELMAN A.C

SIMON FIELDHOUSE
2004

He darted urbanely around the Courts amongst his various cases, patting someone on the head over here, and inserting an elegant stiletto in somebody else's ribs over there; "fin faux et fanfaron" as Talleyrand once said of Metternich at the Congress of Vienna.

I know that is what Talleyrand said, because Tony Larkins told me, and he was there at the time!

As well as conducting his extensive and fashionable practice Mr Street also lectured in the Law School in Company Law. They were vintage days because at the same time Mr A S Mason was lecturing in Equity. I can remember Mr Victor Maxwell in those days taking me to a window on the seventh floor of 180 Phillip Street to observe Mr Mason lecturing across the road in Phillip Street. He said to me "Look at him lecturing in Equity. He looks just like a constipated ostrich. Besides that, he knows nothing about the subject because I beat him at it in the Law School".

At the end of 1964 the student magazine *Blackacre* published epitaphs on various lecturers. Mason's was: "He was a sane and practical man", not a very amusing quotation, one would have thought, from Bernard Shaw. Street's epitaph were the lines of Shakespeare:

> *"The courtier's, soldier's, scholar's eye, tongue, sword,*
> *The expectancy and rose of the fair state,*
> *The glass of fashion and the mould of form"*

A more handsome compliment, one would have thought, though perhaps just hinting at a preference for style over content.

But beginning in 1965 there come ten years of Street's undisputed greatness as an Equity Judge, and by "greatness" I simply mean greatness.

First he disposed of an incredible volume of work: twelve complicated reductions of capital in a day, and three not-short injunction applications in a day. That was nothing to him.

SIR LAURENCE STREET

SIMON FIELDHOUSE 2004

Secondly, he was quick. Few judgments were reserved and all work was disposed of with despatch. Thirdly, his reasons for judgment were comprehensible, felicitously expressed and eminently quotable. His reasons for judgment did not resemble the "position papers" then churned out by the Court of Appeal, lengthy ramblings on matters that their Honours deem to be of current social interest – which have no resemblance to the issues which are actually before the Court.

Nor did his Honour favour that judicial technique of writing pioneered and ultimately perfected by Mr Justice Moffitt, of writing totally verbless sentences.

Fourthly, he had what Sir Robert Megarry said is the greatest possible judicial attribute. I appeared often before him but can hardly remember ever winning a case. Yet I never left his Court feeling any sense of grievance.

Fifthly, his judgments amounted to a significant contribution to equitable learning. This has been recognised overseas as well as in Australia. For example, his judgment in *re Dawson* on a defaulting trustee's obligation to compensate his beneficiaries is the leading authority on that subject quoted in all the main English textbooks, although not with the percipience with which it is quoted in our local textbooks.

In the 1974 Annual Survey of Commonwealth Law Mr Hackney of Wadham College who was well known for his dislike of all judgments of all Judges, wrote of Mr Justice Street's judgment in *re Hilder* on charitable trust to the aged, "This is a splendid contribution to our jurisprudence. We are shown the workings of the law in action. The choice is made between conflicting lines of authority, on the basis that overtly stated social policy, with relevant public law legislation is at the front of the Judge's mind."

And, lastly, by way of example, there is an important decision of his Honour in a case called *re Dinari*. In that case I persuaded his Honour to hold that the now repealed provisions of the Conveyancing Act, dealing with prohibitions on accumulations of income, had no application to settlements made by a corporation. That is a proposition which only a common lawyer would regard as less than riveting. I remember it well for two reasons. One is that it is the only case I can ever remember winning before his Honour. The other is when the decision became known Mr K R Handley, (as he then was) said – with that degree of tact and delicatesse, which I notice from his recent speeches has not abandoned him – that the only reason that decision was given was because neither counsel nor Judge understood the principles involved.

However, it has been approved in recent English decisions and followed regularly both here and abroad.

Then Sir Laurence became Chief Justice. What exactly he did in that office I am not quite certain, because I was never afforded the opportunity of appearing before him. But I understand that he was a dab hand at drafting interjudicial memoranda, and that he devoted a lot of his time to "administration" – which I gather is a buzz word for that policy which prevents barristers drinking coffee in the corridors outside the Courts.

I understand also that he made newly admitted female members of the Bar feel – I was going to say "at home", but I suppose that depends on where they came from.

But one thing he certainly did was to preside over the Court of Criminal Appeal two or three times a week, usually being the Judge who delivered that Court's reasons for judgment. Again one saw the same qualities: quantity of work, speed, elegant, immaculate judgments. And he was almost always correct. There have been very few applications for special leave from the judgments of the Court of Criminal Appeal, and such applications are usually refused. In 1987 there were twelve such applications, ten of which were refused. The previous year there were seventeen out of eighteen applications refused, and two years before that ten out of twelve applications were refused. That is a very impressive record.

I have consulted with persons at the Bar who function in that rather grubby area of the law and have been assured by them, even by the caring and sharing prisoners' rights loony left members of the Bar, that Sir Laurence's behaviour in criminal matters was, amongst other things, warm hearted, humane and even compassionate.

One can only appreciate the particular quality of Sir Laurence Street if one compares him with his successor, Mr Murray Gleeson. At the time of the change-over, there was a feeling at the New South Wales Bar that Charles II was dead and James II had ascended the throne. Differences between their Honours were enumerated and analysed. Of Sir Laurence it was never said that smiling came to him as naturally as flight comes to a porcupine. The physicians never had any difficulty in locating his heart. When he was in command no ice age dawned. In his day the yeti was not the only person who felt comfortable in Court. No signed portrait of Gleeson hangs, or ever will hang, in Kings Cross on the walls of the Bar Coluzzi.

It is not generally known that Murray Gleeson was, amongst other things, the visitor to a convent of nuns. He descended on these hapless women once a week. He inspected their cells to see they contained no bottles of French perfume or books of Protestant theology. He poked his finger into their pillows to ensure they were stuffed with Kapok instead of down. The terrified holy women huddled in their cloisters, praying for him to go away. That is how he developed an extensive Privy Council practice.

I am sure that if Sir Laurence had been the visitor they would have had fears of an entirely different kind.

When Gleeson's appointment was announced the inmates of Long Bay rioted and flung themselves on the barbed wire, raising their heads to heaven and crying out: "Come back Sir Laurence, all is forgiven". Everyone agreed with them.